BEST RELATIONSHIP ADVICES FOR SINGLES, DATING AND DIVORCED

DR. FEMI "GFEM" OGUNJINMI

Published by:
Light Switch Press
PO Box 272847
Fort Collins, CO 80527

Copyright © 2021
ISBN: 978-1-953284-46-4
Printed in the United States of America

(1)   Love is strong medicine. If you took it for the wrong person, you will be sad and broken. But if you took it for the right person, you will be glad and whole.

(2)   Social media is not what broke your relationship. It is the activities you performed on it. The people you are flirting with, sliding into their DMs, and writing seductive comments on their pictures and videos.

(3)   Ladies, it is okay to want a guy who has nice pockets but beware of a guy who spends money on you versus the one who invests in you; the one who views you properly than a property. They can be distinctively two different men.

(4)   A relationship is not something you hop from every few months or years like a job. There are feeling involved. Just because you see another job well advertised and packaged nicely does not mean it is authentic and you are compatible with the company. Do not turn down what you have for a 20 who appears to be 80. Do your research well.

(5)   People often explore Biology (sex) before Chemistry in their relationship. When they have conflict, they use sex as a method to resolve the conflict. However, the problem remains unfixed after the sex. It is imperative to build chemistry, understand how to communicate with

one another so that when there is an issue, you can address it the right way.

(6) If you have a low opinion of yourself, you will tend to go for someone who you think will say yes, the safer bet, the low hanging fruit, someone who does not measure up to a high standard. I encourage you to pick yourself up (self-esteem) and raise your head high. Have self-worth, self-value, and high confidence in yourself.

(7) God's factor is a sine qua non in the process of relationship. Without God's hand in your marriage, it will not be as smooth as it is supposed to be.

(8) You cannot force someone to love you just like you cannot force a horse to drink water. The more you force that person the more he or she withdraws emotionally and physically.

(9) When you go on a date, you want to have a dialogue and not a monologue. Make sure you are not the only one talking and ask how they feel. When you do, they will begin to open up.

(10) Most men are not smart enough to realize the more you elevate your woman, the less available and accessible she is for other men. But when you put her down and belittle her, you make her accessible to anyone she thinks will treat her right and better.

(11)   Bible says a man will leave his mother and father and cleave to his wife. The difference between leaving and cleaving is "C" and that stands for Christ. Invite Christ to your relationship and let him be your foundation.

(12)   If you are not ready to be wrong and corrected, then you are not ready for a relationship.

(13)   For all the newlyweds and those that are about to get married, remember when you say yes on the altar, best believe it that you say yes to a lot of unforeseen things.

(14)   Forgiveness is maturity! It is for people with a big heart.

(15)   The difference between our women today and the ones back in the days is that more women speak up today in their relationship; they convey what they want and dislike. There is nothing wrong with your lady speaking up. She is just being expressive.

(16)   You can tell a woman loves you when her friends say you are no good, but she ignores them by holding on to the word you said to her, "I love you."

(17)   Single people are constantly getting the pressure of marriage from married friends, parents, family, and social media. Do not give in! Take your time to find the right one. There are married folks who are saying silently, 'I will rather be single and happy than keep being married and miserable.'

(18)   One of the powerful tools we possess is our tongue. It can make or break us. Be careful how you use your tongue to talk to the person you are seeing. Elevate and not bash each other with your tongue. People do not forget the horrible things you say to them.

(19)   Most of us never really knew ourselves before the commitment and which is causing so much drama in our relationships. Perhaps you knew yourself does not mean you will not learn a thing or two when you get in a relationship. Do not stop learning and growing. You are responsible for your actions. If you stop learning and growing, you will kill your relationship.

(20)   It is a wrong idea to invest thousands of dollars and time into planning a wedding that lasts few days and invests nothing into a marriage you are expecting to last a lifetime.

(21)   Do not take your baggage to the next relationship. The truth of the matter is you cannot be good for anyone if you are not good for yourself.

(22)   Once you can show a woman you are worth listening to, submitting to, and capable of leading, she will fall deeply in love and do all you say.

(23) Do not be a liability in your relationship. Be an asset. Always contributing and bringing something to the table. A liability has nothing to bargain for and no voice.

(24) If the foundation is solid and you know how to water it, marriage should be one of the best decisions of your life and not the worst.

(25) There is one person out there that will capture your heart and you'll eventually give up every crazy thing you do. Then you will begin to live a better life and create a meaningful future together.

(26) If you do not like what you are receiving from the person you are seeing, then change what you are giving.

(27) Just like you do not choose your parents, your soulmate is not designed by your choosing. Stop telling God who you want and begin to ask who He has for you.

(28) Now and then we get to hear about girls sleeping with married men. I believe that is the beginning of a curse. You say he loves you, but he also loves the woman whom he made a vow to. You want him to divorce his wife and run with you and you think he will do that? If he did, don't you think he can turn around and do the same thing to you? What makes you think you are special, your love is special, your body is special, your characters are better? I admonish you to find your own

single man and stop being used by married men. Do not allow yourself to destroy another woman's home. It does not matter if he is the one coming to approach you. Give yourself self-respect and decency. What goes around can come back around.

(29) Do not look for love at first sight because it might just be lust at first sight. The best thing to look for is "Friend-ship" at first sight because that is the fundamental of love and it is what you need first. You need to be able to click as a friend, hold nothing back, and open to share your experiences.

(30) A relationship where you both think and do things for one another is bound to last.

(31) Not knowing your relationship status with an individual is like expecting a GPS to take you to your destination without putting in your starting point. You are going no-where!

(32) A relationship is not about what the outside culture says, it is?: about the culture you develop in your relationship. Do not be influenced by traditions. Create your own cul-ture that works for both of you.

(33) Only hurt people hurt people. Only unhappy people make others unhappy.

(34) There is one common issue I see with those that are dating and that is "Happiness." Everyone wants to be happy and looking for that one person for the job. When you live a life waiting for others to make you happy, you become vulnerable and not always satisfied. What you need to do is to tap into your internal happiness and that will change the outcome of your love life.

(35) Let your mind be at rest finding your bone. You will have your male partner in due time. The word has already gone out that "…none shall lack her mate…" Isaiah 34:16

(36) Inability to forgive one another leaves no room for growth. Without forgiveness, we really cannot move on. It is hard to forgive but it is the best thing to do.

(37) Do not get disappointed when you are dating someone under 27yrs of age and he or she is acting immature and making irrational decisions. Science says your brain is not fully formed until you are 27yrs old.

(38) Sometimes in life, you must drop the zero and get with a hero. Other times, it is best to help make the zero a hero. May God give you the spirit of discernment to know what decision to make.

(39) Do not use each other's weakness to pull each other and destroy one another. Rather use it to lift and strengthen each other.

(40) The best part about love is fighting through your disagreement/argument quickly and bouncing back to a peaceful state again.

(41) Do not create a problem by trying to solve a problem. For example: walking out on each other during an argument can lead to an accident on your way out or lead to falling in the hands of someone else.

(42) Do not marry a man because he has a television (a euphemism for anything shinning that he possesses). Marry a man because he can tell you his vision, you can see yourself in his vision, and eventually, you will both have the television.

(43) If you are not ready to make the sacrifice then you are not ready to be in a relationship, talk less about becoming a parent. Sacrifice is one of the key requirements of becoming a partner and parent. Learn to make a sacrifice now and then if you want to experience the latent joy, peace, and longevity of a relationship.

(44) Me, Mine, and I - The trinity that destroys a relationship. I want this, I want that, it is my money, it is my house, or it is my car. Stay away from that mindset and

phrases. They will negatively affect your relationship. Everything you own in a relationship belongs to both of you. Two shall be joined together and become one.

(45) The 3 Big C's that might be missing in your relationship: Creativity, Commitment, & Conversation. Work on these pillars and your relationship will be rock solid.

(46) Marriage has nothing to do with age but maturity. Though maturity most time comes with age people who are old are sometimes as confused as young people. Jesus says not everyone is matured enough to live a married life. He did not put an age on it. Adam and Eve were created as matured beings (Genesis 2:22-24) to depict the profile of marriage and that is a reason God did not spare them of consequences for not following his instructions.

(47) Many are experiencing fiery trials in their relationship and they are hoping for a fairy tale. The attributed cause of the problem is that people marry to love and not love to marry. Do not be in a rush for marriage if love is not present. Hoping to find love when you get married is wishful thinking. It is good to be proactive. Your foundation of love can help you get through difficult times in the relationship. But if love never existed, you would wish to leave the relationship.

(48)   It breaks my heart when ladies think they can meet the love of their life at a club. I threw parties for so many years and I attended other people's parties before God delivered me. There was not a single time I went to a party or threw a party thinking I was going to meet the love of my life there. I was throwing and going to parties for fun. Even when I spoke to guys coming to my parties, they were coming there to fish girls and make these girls their conquest. I am sorry to lay this truth out. The club is not an ideal place people look for wives and husbands. Though there might be some people who could have found the love of their life there, do not get me wrong but they are not many in the world. Not too many success stories of such.

(49)   A relationship built on lies and fakery is bound for a lot of troubles. If the car, house, money, clothes, job profession, job title, or other accomplishments are not yours, then do not claim them. Telling someone that you have what you do not have is pure lies.

(50)   People who come to your life are either a blessing or a lesson. Whatever they choose to be is for your benefit, growth, and endurance. Never feel down or disappointed for anything. Just keep it moving.

(51)   If you plan to break up with someone you are seeing, that means one or a combination of these things has tak-

en place: (a) the love you once had is gone (b) there is something more powerful than the love you had that is tearing the relationship apart (c) there was no love from the beginning of the relationship, to begin with.

(52) Work might be stressful, the job may be a loss, the business might be crashing, you might be failing classes, money might be tough, your critics might be blaming you, bills may be difficult to pay but when you come home and you have a partner that makes you forget the issues and provide support, that's when you know you've got the right partner and it's important to search for such person while you are still single.

(53) Your relationship is not beyond repair. It is either one or two of these things that are happening (a) You have or have not discovered the solution (b) You do not want to repair it.

(54) It is not about how much you fight but how well you learn from your fight that you can prevent the same fight again.

(55) Three daily habits of successful couples: Pray together, Play together, & Plan together.

(56) If you are still angry, bitter, and disappointed about your past relationship then you cannot successfully handle a

brand-new relationship with satisfaction, happiness, peace, and excitement.

(57) You must get in a relationship with someone willing to do for you as much as you are willing to do in return. A relationship is a two-way street.

(58) A successful relationship is not the result of one act of service. It is the repetition and consistent service you provide to one another that gives the result you desire.

(59) Pledge daily to be faithful to your relationship. Do not be a faith fool!

(60) The more time you spend together, the better you understand each other and reduce conflicts. People grow apart because they do not spend time together. You can be living in the same house and still grow apart because you are not spending time together.

(61) Ladies understand that you are a good thing. Whoever wants to marry you as a wife has found a good thing and obtains favor from God. Now even though you are a good thing, you 'cannot be good for everyone. Only a prostitute is good for everyone and you are not one. So, it is okay if he says he does not want to rock with you anymore. You just wait for the right man, the flesh of your flesh, bone of your bone to come and take your hand in marriage.

(62) The combination of a man who lacks wisdom and patience and a woman who lacks good manners and cannot control her mouth will damage their relationship.

(63) The frustration I see with single folks is that they meet so many potentials that have what they are looking for, but the potentials are missing one thing they cannot compromise. I have been there; I had so many potential girls but none of them was qualified, so I waited till I found my soul mate. Understand that your soul mate will have what you cannot compromise so wait for him or her.

(64) Can the two work together except they agree? A successful relationship is a result of two determined people to make it work.

(65) In this modern world, the phrase 'for better for worse' does not exist in everyone's dictionary. The phrase is based on what the individual considers worse. Couples and aspiring couples should have a dialogue on what is considered worse and what the threshold of worse is to prevent separation and divorce.

(66) With or without marriage, you should still become who God has destined you to become. Do not let marriage be your destination.

(67) If you let anger control you, it can destroy all you have worked hard for including the new relationship. Control it do not let it control you.

(68) When you expect someone to meet your requirements or standards, but you do not meet the same requirements, you are creating a double standard. Do not demand what you do not demand yourself.

(69) As single Christian ladies and men, do not be apprehensive to ask God to reveal if the person you are talking to is the right "One." Proverbs 3:5-6 says, "Trust in the Lord with all thine heart and lean not unto thine own understanding. In all thy ways acknowledge him, and he shall direct thy paths."

(70) If you are expecting your man to know what you need & want at your desire time, well, well, well, he is not God. He is man-made of clay. He does not know what is in your mind. Just communicate what you want and need. Keep the situation simple.

(71) You have so many brothers and sisters in church playing an instrument, singing, ushering, protocoling, active in one department or the other. It does not mean they are the right ones for you. Some of them serve God with their mouth but not with their heart. Their characters are worse than unbelievers. That is why you must check

their spirit. The church is meant for people to get healed and not everyone is healed yet.

(72) You want a guy who makes six figures and then he turns around and spends the money on other girls. You want a man who has a six-pack, well built, and then he boxes you like iron Mike Tyson. There is nothing wrong with having a man with money and a nice physique but there is more to superficial things when it comes to being in a healthy and satisfying relationship.

(73) There are gold-digger women and so there are gold-digger men. They are in it to get your money. You pay their bills, pay for the date, cook, and clean for them. Beware of them.

(74) Some people do not have bad characters or behaviors. Past relationships turned them this way. I encourage you to have a change of heart because this new you might be hurting you from securing the ideal relationship.

(75) Do not marry someone who will decrease your value. Marry someone who will increase your value and support your vision.

(76) You need to become a complete, independent person before and while you are in a relationship otherwise you will become a burden.

(77)   There are different types of love. The one we most think of Eros: it is the sexual love that is most akin to our modern construct of romantic love. This kind of love does not last and is based on so many conditions and self-interest (i.e., looks, money, care, respect, etc.) The only type of love that is most important and will last is Agape love (unconditional love). It is based on zero conditions. If couples have that for one another, they will be able to prevent/and or endure all things.

(78)   Women are more emotional beings and sensitive than men while men are more on the analytical side. Therefore, you need to allow your woman to tell you how she is feeling. A woman can sense troubles from miles away. But for you as a man, even if the trouble is under your nose you may not feel it.

(79)   All men are dogs as they say. If that is true, then you need yourself a trained one who listens and obeys his master (God). You need a good dog who will not eat everything he sees because all he sees is in one thing that he eats.

(80)   The primary problem of relationships all over the world is that they operate relationship without information (Revelation). The operation of a thing without revelation (information) leads to frustration and destruction. Information begets operation.

(81) A healthy relationship is like eating something nutritious to be healthy. Quite often we do not like eating salad because we do not have a sense of taste for it, but we eat it regardless because we want to be healthy. So is relationship. There are right things you must do in a relationship that you are not naturally inclined to do. But you must do them to make your relationship healthy.

(82) If you get mad when the person you are seeing talks about his or her ex, then you probably not healed about what could have happened between your partner and their ex.

(83) Beauty can attract someone to you. Character is what can make the person say.

(84) If you cannot be satisfied by one woman then no number of women can satisfy you. What you need is self-discipline, the Holy Spirit, and fear of God.

(85) If your definition of Mr. Right or Mrs. Right is a perfect person, sorry the person does not exist on this planet. What you might get is Mr. Almost Right or Ms. Pretty Close. God is the perfect one.

(86) While you are single, dating or in a relationship, develop an interest in different things. Interest makes you interesting. Nobody wants to go out on a date or be with someone boring.

(87) A relationship is not about getting something from one another; it is about building something together.

(88) Improving your life automatically improves your relationship. Your relationship reflects who you are; If you and your partner can both grow together, your relationship will become a good by-product.

(89) Having a complete true love is when the receiver is more like the giver.

(90) Being single is not a curse. You are not a second-class Christian in the eyes of God. You are a complete & awesome individual.

(91) Stop crying over who left you! In life, you either say hello or goodbye. Tell that sucker goodbye. Hello is coming.

(92) Waiting on the Lord does not mean you should stop dating or seeing people and expecting God to drop the one at your doorstep. A relationship does not work like that. It is like expecting God to bless you with a job and you are home not applying for jobs, putting your resume together, and interviewing. You got to play your part and let God handle the rest.

(93) It is easy to fall in love but hard to deal with a break-up. Guard your heart & become vulnerable for only those who deserve it.

(94) You should see single life as a season to get your dreams out, get in focus with your life, start your business, own a company and when that right person comes along you can build a bigger company and chase bigger dreams together. Being ambitious is sexy.

(95) You may have to let them GO so that they can GROW. It could also mean you may be the one to GO so that you can GROW.

(96) A relationship is one university you never graduate from. The moment you stop learning, the moment you stop growing.

(97) A man is indeed a provider. But not only so much about finances. A man should provide wisdom, ideas, a solution to problems, guidance, emotional intelligence, friendship, vision, camaraderie, mental toughness, and courage. The functionality of a man is way more than the bacon he brings home.

(98) Every relationship is a work in progress. Keep working on it so that you can enjoy it.

(99) If it is all about what is in between the legs and on the face that gets people to be chosen as a wife, all the prostitutes will be married. It takes more than the body to be chosen as a wife.

(100)   One effective principle to a successful and happy relationship is conversation. Arouse each other's mind and not just body. Have a dialogue and not a monologue.

(101)   Submission is not what one person does in a relationship. It is what both parties do for one another as respect and honor to the commitment and viability of the marriage and ultimately to God who joined them together.

(102)   Submission is not slavery. It is smartly putting your power under the control of another person for the goal of the relationship. You should always submit to one another to keep your relationship viable.

(103)   Here are three important things to consider before leaping into a new relationship: (a) Attraction. It comes in many forms; both physical and mental. Attraction is mostly the prelude to a relationship. We are first attracted to people we fall in love with. The body shape, outfit, and beauty draw us close to them. Also, you want to be connected mentally. It is important for the conversation to be interesting and have things in common. This will excite you to always want to be around them. (b) Attitude. While we look at the outward physiological composition of the person, it's imperative to also seek what's on the inside(attitude/

character) of the individual. The character (which is often shown by a set of behaviors) is who the person is and ultimately determines if the person will treat you right. Pay close attention to it. (c) Asset. Examine the person's lifestyle, experience, goals, and skill set to determine if they will be an asset or a liability to your life. Everyone is not equipped to add value to your life. A liability individual will make your life miserable and not enjoyable. While an asset will make your life interesting and pleasant.

(104) Every relationship has a problem. At the same time, it is important not to give power to the problem by talking too much about it. Be about a solution! When you study successful entrepreneurs and companies, they barely spend most of their time talking about problems; they invest most of their energy coming up with multiple solutions to fix the problem. If the solution you previously proposed does not work out, then strategize a new one. Do not stress your relationship with complaints. It will not get you anywhere. It will always push your partner away from you. Nobody wants to be around negative energy.

(105) Money cannot buy love, but it can make you enjoy love. The presence of money will make you discover another level of love for your partner. The absence

of it can turn to serial arguments, anger, frustration, irritation, and annoyance.

(106)   Any man who has no patience cannot enjoy his woman.

(107)   You know how to be treated but you choose to be treated in the wrong way. Do not blame the person treating you badly. It is you accepting and tolerating the bad behavior. If you do not like what you are receiving, then change what you are giving.

(108)   The challenge in a relationship is one person doing the right thing and the other doing the wrong thing. It will be good if it takes one person to make a good relationship. Unfortunately, it takes two people. Keep working on it.

(109)   A forced relationship leads to an easy break-up. Do not force anyone to love you. Let love happens organically.

(110)   Holding hands, kissing, singing love songs, texting one another throughout the day, are great medicines to vitalize your union.

(111)   Your breakup is not worth worrying and crying over but rejoicing over. It was designed that way so that you can discover the real deal.

(112)   Ladies preserve the cookie jar!!! It is important. Sex can affect your decision-making, turns you into a desperate person, blinds you from seeing his games, prevents you from dumping his angry/abusive nature, and keeps you in the relationship even when he is treating you badly. The same goes for the man. It can make you abusive and controlling towards the girl. You may not even know that it has a direct correlation with your erratic behavior(s).

(113)   Men enjoy respect just as much as women enjoy love. It is the DNA that cannot be altered. Give each other what is expected.

(114)   Do not chase after him; you having to call, text, set update and he has given failed promises, are signs that he is not into you. Men are built like a chaser. We hunt for what we want and if he is not hunting for you then he does not want you. Hunting is what makes us alive. It is the thrill and excitement for us. You want a man who is interested, excited to hunt and chase you down. If he wants to put you in his life, he will put you there. You do not have to fight for it.

(115)   It is a great mistake when your woman has an issue and your first approach as a man is trying to solve it. Your first approach should be to listen with empathy. You need to first gain her trust that you care about

her feelings, emotions and that you clearly understand what she is going through.

(116)   10% of conflict comes from a difference of opinion. The remaining 90 percent is from delivery and tonation. If you want to avoid the majority of the conflicts in your relationship you will need to control the 90 percent.

(117)   The loneliness you feel is not because you need a partner; it is a reflection that you have not discovered your purpose and/or living in your purpose. If you are busy working on your purpose, your mind will be preoccupied and will not feel like you need a partner. You will realize that while you are working on your purpose, that partner you are seeking will seek you or meet each other while working on the field just like Boaz met Ruth.

(118)   Quality wedding rings do not determine the success of a marriage. A new house does not produce a new marriage. A new outfit does not produce a new you. You can get a new car but if it is the same old engine, you will receive the same old experience. If you get into a new relationship and bring your old negative mindset, you will receive an old negative result. What you need is to have a renewed mind for out of it will produce a new you and desired outcome.

(119)   The number 3 is a significant number that produces a balanced result. Your relationship requires the marriage of three people to be effective, balanced, and sustainable. Those three are God, Yourself, & Spouse. You should marry God first, yourself second, and your spouse as the third partner.

(120)   The reason you are not listening to each other during conflict is that you are both pointing fingers at each other without admitting first what you did to contribute to the problem and what you are going to do next time to prevent it from happening.

(121)   There is a threshold to what a woman can take. If you keep playing with her heart she will just get up and leave your butt one day.

(122)   Being single is a state of pursuing personal agenda, focusing on self-purpose, personal goals, renewing oneself, working on oneself, developing oneself, redefining oneself, and improving oneself. You do all these so that you can add more to the marriage and become who God wants you to be as an individual. If you get married and you do not continue working on yourself, you will end up losing yourself and the relationship. Being single should not just exist before your relationship, it should happen throughout the lifetime of your relationship.

(123)   Do not make a permanent decision over a temporary situation. Beware of the devil that tries to trick you and whisper in your ears to break your relationship. Just because things are rough right now does not mean they will be like that forever. Every relationship has its challenging moment when it looks as if it is over, and the problem cannot be fixed. Just because your friend's relationship looks happy does not mean they have not had their tough moments. The emotions you are feeling will soon pass away like a cloud. Seek God and counseling.

(124)   Who should I be with? Be with someone who can help you become a better version of yourself and fulfill the plans of God for your life.

(125)   Do not put the burden of your happiness on the person you are dating and do not let anyone make you feel responsible for their happiness. Their happiness is solely their responsibility.

(126)   If you love someone, you will make all the sacrifices to keep them. If you are not making the sacrifice, then it is either you do not love them, or your love is not deep enough. Do not fool around with him or her playing with your heart and head. If they are not making the sacrifice to correct their issues, bad behavior, and action then they are not in love with you, or the

love is just not deep enough to make the necessary changes to keep you.

(127) What is the difference between a man who wants to play you and the one who wants to be with you? They both tell you they love you, buy you material things, show you signs of care, and show you off to their friends. But guess what? a player will not take you home to meet his parent(s) and introduce you as his woman to marry. May you be led to the hands of the one who wants to marry you.

(128) If your woman is mad at you that means she believed in you, but you broke her trust, and she is disappointed. If she is complaining and asking questions, it means she still cares. But if she is not talking and just allowing things to slide, that means she is giving up, or she has given up on you and possibly getting ready to leave your butt. Act before it gets to that moment.

(129) You are single because God is working on the person who will be deserving of you. Do not rush the process.

(130) A relationship is about adding value to each other. That is how God created us to be. God made Eve add value to Adam. And God created Adam to make sure he added value to Eve. It is fruitless walking in or holding on to a relationship that will not serve and elevate you.

(131)   Your singleness and dating struggle might be a result of doing too much, too soon, and for free. Take your time to know the person. Most things that are given freely and too soon are not appreciated and valued.

(132)   If you take your mind from always building and perfecting yourself, you will become a problem in every relationship you get into. Before getting and while you are in a relationship, it is important to exponentially develop yourself morally, academically, mentally, physically, financially, and spiritually.

(133)   It is interesting what causes argument in a relationship when you expect your partner to magically get into your head and know exactly what should make you happy when you do not know what brings you happiness. Partners put too much expectation on each other, and it is a reflection that they do not fully understand themselves before getting into a relationship. Take time to know yourself, satisfy yourself, comfortable being with yourself, and loving yourself before deciding on spending your whole life with someone else.

(134)   One of the integral components of a relationship is "Forgiveness." If you cannot forgive the person you are dating and/or yourself, you are setting your relationship for failure. The end of a hardened heart is destruction. Ask Pharaoh! The Lord hardened his heart

to lead him and his army to destruction at the Red Sea. What a sad ending. I do not wish the same for you. Have a forgiven heart.

(135)   The idea of a new relationship feels good, but it will end up like the previous one if you do not water it.

(136)   To have a great relationship, you need two things:

(137)   (a) The knowledge and tools to bring about the change you want. That is why reading books and attending seminars are important to acquire the knowledge that will shed light on your difficulties and give you the steps to overcome them. (b) You need the drive to implement the acquired knowledge and make things work.

(138)   Sex will not solve a problem that is not sex-related. Address your issues without sex.

(139)   People do not fall out of love; they usually fall out of forgiveness. When people break up over matters, it is typically they do not have any more energy and heart of forgiving the other person for their misbehavior(s).

(140)   Sleep is for peace and not for pain. Resolve your matter with the person you are seeing before going to sleep.

(141)   Communicate with the person by (a) Validating their feelings; ask how they feel about what they are addressing you on (especially if they are dissatisfied about your action).(b) By regurgitating or paraphrasing to them what they say, suggests you are listening.

(142)   Men should learn to exercise patience when interacting with their women. A man without patience cannot successfully enjoy his relationship. Same for women.

(143)   Choose your partner by Purpose (God's choice for you that aligns with his purpose for your life) and not by your Preference (earthly desires and limited vision).

(144)   Single ladies, what is your buzz? What is the word on the street about you? A bad buzz such as bad character can hold you back from being approached by the ideal man. God bless your eyelash, Brazilian hair, and all the makeup you put on. But if the makeup of your character is not attractive, it may deter you from getting a husband. Work on your character and build a good buzz.

(145)   You must conduct a "Background Check" on your potential spouse before saying "I Do." A background check will reveal the wolf in sheepskin. Do not marry based on face value. Many people are acting while single. You may be marrying the person because of his/her wealth, family wealth,

posh lifestyle thinking this will end your challenges but not knowing it will only compound it. Perform a spiritual, financial, health, family, lifestyle, and background check. This will reduce a lot of challenges you could potentially run into that afflict numerous relationships.

(146) The more I coach singles the more I realize everyone is becoming political in their conversation that is creating conflict. Yes, you have freedom of speech but do not just invoke it on your partner by being insensitive. If you want to get the best result from your conversation, you should speak with caution, respect, and tact otherwise your freedom of speech will create conflict and problems.

(147) What gets a man's attention does not always earn his respect and what turns a man's head may not always turn his heart. Be wise not to misinterpret a man's behavior or action towards you.

(148) Two of the strong factors that a Christian marriage requires to be viable are the Presence of God and Money. Money is a defense! When challenges of life offend you, you need money as a defense. And when the spiritual challenges of life offend you, you need the presence of God to defend you.

(149)   I see this play out many times when single ladies give their bodies to a guy as a sign to show they like him and are interested in dating or being with him. The guy, however, does not have the same reason for giving his body. He gives because he wants your body in exchange. He is not emotionally attached. But you give because you want more than sex (his heart, relationship, commitment, time, loyalty, etc.) That is a revelation of a relationship for you ladies. Be wise!

(150)   It is good to be spiritual but doing it in the absence of not taking good care of yourself, not dressing the part, and looking all rough/unclean will inhibit your chance of being approached by a prospect. Attraction is the antecedent that excites anyone to be interested in you and to discover all the other great qualities you possess. Be spiritual and at the same time look attractive! You do not serve unclean God.

(151)   Do not get under somebody to get over somebody. That is the biggest mistake you can make when trying to get over a past relationship. Avoid sleeping with somebody or jumping into a new relationship as a method to get over the old relationship. The new relationship will not last because the foundation is wrong and, you are using the person for your agenda.

(152)   Can you fall out of love? Yes, and it is possible to fall back in love. Do you know how many times we have fallen out of love with Jesus and we still go back? Sometimes you are highly motivated to serve God, sharing His works, spending time in His presence, reading your scriptures, appreciating Him daily. Then suddenly you stopped for whatever reason you know and then six months later you go back to loving Him again by doing the same thing you used to do when you were in love with Him. The same is with the relationship you have with your partner. You can fall out of love when you stop loving, caring, appreciating, worshipping, and spending time with each other. And you can fall back in love by doing the aforementioned (loving, caring, spending time with each other, etc.).

(153)   If you are looking for a life partner, do not just look for someone that will cover you physically. But someone who will also fulfill the spiritual assignment in your life. The purpose of marriage is bigger than the two of you and your children.

(154)   The expectation of your new relationship is mostly hinged on the experience of your past relationship. You need to evaluate and heal from your experience so that you do not treat your NEXT like your EX.

(155)   Sometimes the person who hurts you did not even know they did. And you are over there losing sleep. Listen, sleep is for PEACE and not for being PISSED. Perhaps you wish to hurt them so that they can feel what you feel, read this quote from Beyonce that says, "Love is an endless act of forgiveness. Forgiveness is me giving up the right to hurt you for hurting me." Learn to forgive and move on with life quickly.

(156)   A college is a great place where you can meet people, find a mate, and yet most relationships established in college do not last till marriage. Why? most people dating in college are not dating with the purpose of marriage in mind and they are not ready for the responsibilities of marriage right after college. That means you must understand this information, be logical, and make a decision on why you want to date in the first place including identifying the goal of it and what is in it for you.

(157)   Fight and issues often get unresolved while dating primarily because you are picking the wrong time to discuss it. Consult with the person you are seeing for a perfect time. Do not let your emotions, anger, and frustration dictate it.

(158)   If there is no SACRIFICE, there is no LOVE. It is as simple as ABC. Sacrifice is giving up something

in exchange and/or demonstration for the greater love you have for your partner. If you love someone, you will make all the sacrifices to keep them.

(159)   I know the relationship can be complicated. To unravel its complexity here is a simple formula approach: Know who you marry, Respect who you marry, Love who you marry, and Support who you marry.

(160)   This is the mindset and what partners should tell each other instead of proving to be right to each other. "I'll rather tell you I'm sorry than proving to be right because I value you and our relationship more than being right.

(161)   Every man becomes a baby around the right woman. No man is that strong that he cannot become tame. When he finds that special one, he lowers his guard. If your man is not your baby, then he is either not your man or you have not discovered what possibly could make him your baby.

(162)   It is okay to naturally desire a compliment from another human being, but it is not okay to feel something must be wrong with you if you are not getting it. Believe that you are perfectly beautiful and attractive without a word of compliment from anyone.

(163)   Do not let your singleness frustrate you that it makes you thirsty and leads you to the path of desperation. A rushed relationship can lead to a rushed divorce. Take your time.

(164)   Any man can change. He just needs to make up his mind to change, be touched by God, and do it for a good reason.

(165)   The quickest way to get played is when you are too quick to open your heart and legs while you should be opening your real estate (mind) to assess the person, their character, and lifestyle. If you want to understand who you are dealing with, cut out the benefits and the real person will show up.

(166)   A man is either playing you or planning with you. Get a man that will plan with you. Put you on his agenda, goals, and future. If you are not in his plan, then you are just in his panty's plan.

(167)   Thank God for the blessing and lesson every relationship brings. Living in the past does nothing other than preventing you from realizing and actualizing your potential. Use your past to encourage yourself to be better today and forever.

(168)   Your past relationship is a place of reference, not residence. Do not live there.

(169) If you are scared to tell a man you want a committed relationship and afraid to ask the following: What are we? Do you love me? Then you should be scared to be in that relationship. You are allowing yourself to be manipulated and become a string along. Please do not be afraid to ask regardless of the response you do not want to hear. It is better to know how he feels about you now if he wants to be in a committed relationship with you than expend time and energy that you should have expended on the right person and right relationship. The same advice goes for men.

(170) It is important to understand that there will be challenges when you get into a relationship. Do not think there will not be. However, it is better to go through them with the right person than the wrong one. Take your time to find the right person.

(171) At times God does not want to communicate through a coach, counselor, or Pastor. He wants to communicate with you directly. So often we seek guidance from counselors, coaches, or pastors on relationship matters, but you are forgetting that they are not always going to be present. Perhaps have the perfect answer. You need to start developing a personal relationship with God so you can hear directly what He's saying concerning who you are about to marry. Some

of the challenges you are facing can be solved with a single word from God directly to you.

(172)   You do not need a man who is a knight and shining armor. You need a man who is covered with the Armor of God. And then you will see the true Knight and shining armor he is. What God has for you sometimes does not come in the obvious package you are asking for. God must open your eyes in a different way to crack open the package and see the true content in it. Humans are the most pretentious creatures. They make themselves look rich, but they are not. They make themselves look like they have it all together, but they do not. Open your eyes to see the true content in the container and not just the container.

(173)   You are single today and unhappy not because God wants you to be single but because you lost a good man or woman when you had them. You could not straighten yourself up when you were given the opportunities to. You could not make the tough decision, which was the right decision. You were lusting after someone else instead to be loving after your partner. You were playing in someone else's yard instead of your partner's yard. Because you wanted to follow the crowd and do the same thing your friends were doing. If you were given another opportunity again, do not blow it up.

(174)   How can you say that you are compatible with the person? People have a different interpretation of compatibility when it comes to relationships. Does it mean what I like she must like? she must look the same as I do or what I do not as she must dislike as well? That is what we think compatibility is all about. I want you to think in terms of a partnership. In partnership no one knows it all, no one has it all. Everyone comes with their unique gift and strength, which complement the weakness or deficiency of the other party. That means what I do not have, the other person has. And what I do not know the other person knows or perhaps what I do know but do not know as much as they do. That is compatibility.

(175)   The best way to deal with a break-up is to: (a) Identify your fault; what you did wrong, how you contributed to the demise of the relationship. Look at the person in the mirror and get the lessons from it. Do not point the finger. If you are pointing a finger and not looking at what you did wrong, you will likely make the same mistake again (b) Get rid of the person's contact from your phone. It is the best method to get rid of temptation because you can be tempted to reach out to the person to say hi, to have closure and that can make you feel all emotional again. (c) Start to work on yourself. Work on who you were before you met

the person. If that means that you were working on your goals, academics, dreams, your health, and enjoying life before you met them. If not, then start doing them now.

(176) Comparison is what people do in a relationship that does not realize is slowly killing their partner and hurting their relationship. If you must compare your partner to someone else to get them to do something or change, you already lost their interest to change. It creates more damage than what you are trying to fix in the first place. The best method is to consistently explain what you want them to do, and they will eventually change.

(177) If you do not have standards, you will tolerate everything and when you tolerate everything, you will attract anyone, which is not good for you.

(178) Money is not everything, but it is necessary for building a relationship and a family.

(179) If you are arguing, complains, and non-physical fight with your partner now and then does not mean your relationship is bad or you should break up. It should not stop you from loving one another as well. It just indicates that you guys still have more learning to do about each other. And it is better to learn than not to.

Learning is part of your growth. If you are not learning, then you are not growing.

(180)   Life is about a relationship. No one can make it without the help of another. Life is just designed that way. However, it is deemed important to know as well that a wrong relationship will produce a bad result for you. It will slow you down or derail you from the right path to your goals. How can you know you are with the wrong person? The answer is in the question you ask yourself, "With this person in my life what do they have me thinking, feeling, doing, reading, saying, planning, where do they have me going? Am I progressing? If there is no positive answer and those answers do not align with your morals and Godly values, then you are in a relationship with the wrong person. When you are in a relationship with the wrong person, you end up where they are going.... not a good place.

(181)   If you are having an issue with someone you are dating, and they reacted in a way that made you wonder what just happened? You noticed the issue is so minute, but the magnitude of their reaction is bigger than the issue itself. You start to question yourself what did I do wrong? Listen to me, you did not do anything wrong. They are not reacting to you. They are reacting based on the experience they had before

with the person they had it with before you being in the picture. It is not you; it is them. You just triggered something that looks like their past situation. You are being treated by their wounds, their past, that they never dealt with and healed from. What you need to do is to have a dialogue with them where the reaction and attitude are coming from. Who hurts them in the past? Is it their friend, ex, father, mother, or relatives? Get to the bottom of it and you will find answers.

(182)   Stop breaking up and hopping from one relationship to the next just because the person offended or hurt you. The bitter truth about a relationship is that any partner you choose will hurt your feelings and you will do the same either intentionally or unintentionally. That is why the word, 'I'm sorry,' 'Pls Forgive me' and, 'It won't happen again' exist. Every relationship is the same; we are all experiencing the same issue (hurt and offense). The difference is the level, the intensity, and the rate at which we offend each other deliberately or not deliberately. Every relationship is not worth it but does not make it a habit that you always take the highway when things are not smooth. Learn to deal with the problem with your partner. Address the issue and fix it. The grass is not always greener on the other side.

(183)   Who Should You Marry? What I recommend is to marry your life-assignment partner. What does that mean? God gives you a life partner based on your life assignment. God does not care about your beauty or physiological preference. Adam did not have a say in the descriptions of who (Eve) God made for him. He was put to sleep during the process. Also, Eve was created and called 'helpmate' after God gave Adam his life assignments and vision. The purpose or the life assignments you are both created must first align and congruent to God's will. If you can figure out your life assignment early or already in it before being in a relationship, it can help you to choose the right partner and eliminate the wrong prospect.

(184)   Every right relationship should be able to bring you two things: Blessing and Lesson. If you are only getting one, then it is either you are not in the right relationship or you are not maximizing the relationship for what it should be. You should be able to learn from your partner and at the same time be blessed by their presence in the relationship. It is like walking with God; we learn from our relationship with him and get blessed by him.

(185)   Ladies should not be thirsty for a man. That is the number one mistake ladies are making. It is not your role to ask a man out or pursue him. Instead, make

yourself (everything about you not just your look) attractive, positioned, and you will be pursued.

(186) The frustration I see with single folks is that they meet so many potentials that have what they are looking for, but the potentials are missing one thing they cannot compromise. Your soul mate will have what you cannot compromise so wait for him or her.

(187) It is imperative to understand that in the construct of love relationships in modern-day society, there is no such thing as male roles or female roles. They are just roles and whoever is gifted at the roles should perform them. What differentiates us and determines our roles is a gift, not our gender. It is our intrinsic interest, value, knowledge, capacity, and skill set we possess to perform the roles. Empowering each other as partners will spur economic growth, create power balance, increase everyone's self-happiness, and make you a better family.

(188) Communication to the person you are dating is not just talking. It involves having the right timing, a positive tone of voice, being kind, compassionate, showing empathy, and not be sarcastic.

(189) You can walk away from a relationship but do not walk away from yourself. You are matter. Do not give up on yourself. Self-love and care are important. Nev-

er lose yourself. You are the real deal. The more you love yourself the more love you can give to others. The more you care for yourself the more you understand how to care for others. You cannot give others what you do not have. Practice self-love and care. It is not a selfish act. Rather it is what will eventually position you with enough capacity to help your partner and children.

(190) The argument is not worth losing your relationship over. Trying to win an argument can sometimes cause you to lose your relationship. I believe the relationship is worth holding on to than the offense you are keeping. You either choose to be happy or to be right. Just saying "sorry" is sometimes all it takes to calm the tension and resolve the argument.

(191) Be with somebody who can help you become a better version of yourself and fulfill the plans of God for your life.

(192) You want a guy who makes six figures and then he turns around and spends the money on other girls. You want a man who has a six-pack, well built, and the boxes you like iron Mike Tyson. There is nothing wrong with having a man with money and a nice physique but there is more to superficial things when

it comes to being in a healthy and satisfying relationship.

(193)   Your relationship needs spontaneity. One of the best
things you can do to spice up your relationship is to be
spontaneous. Do not let your relationship be routine
and boring. By being spontaneous you have a way of
surprising your partner, lifting their spirit, increasing
their dopamine level, and drawing them to you. Find
something spontaneous to do for your partner today.

(194)   You cannot change a relationship. Really? Yea. you
can only change the people living in the relationship.
You need to understand that relationship is not an ob-
ject you can modify. It is just a 'word' to describe people in a communal engagement. So, it is the people
in the relationship that can bring about the change. If
you change, then your relationship will reflect it.

(195)   If your definition of Mr. Right or Ms. Right is a per-
fect person; sorry they do not exist on this planet.
What you might get is Mr. Almost Right or Ms. Pretty
Close. God is the perfect one.

(196)   Being single is not a curse. You are not a second-class
Christian in the eyes of God. You are a complete and
awesome individual.

(197)   Anger can keep us from developing a spirit pleasing to God and our partner. Have you ever been proud that you did not strike out and say what was really on your mind to your partner? Self-control is good, but Christ wants us to practice thought-control as well. You cannot get to self-control if you have not fully executed thought-control effectively. Anger is a dangerous emotion to have that can threaten to leap out of control, lead to violence, emotional hurt, and increased mental stress. Take control of your thought so that you can better handle your anger instead of your anger handling you.

(198)   Forgive the person you are seeing if you want the relationship to get better and progress.

(199)   Do not be intimidated if the person you are dating is smarter in areas you are not and do not let that drive you to competition either. A relationship is designed to complement one another, not compete. It is a partnership you are forming, and in partnership, no one knows it all. Embrace and celebrate the competence of one another. Your relationship will thrive better when you do.

(200)   Do not threaten to end a relationship with someone you are dating to get him or her to do what you want. It is an unethical, immature, not biblical, and wrong

approach that can frustrate your partner to give up. You may end up regretting it if the partner accepted the break-up. Talk through what you want, explain what you want, share how you feel about how he or she is treating you, and get help. It is a better and safer method that could produce a better result than a threat.

(201) Three essential elements should be present with someone you want to spend the rest of your life with. (a) Physical: You are attracted to their aesthetic, style, physique, and personalities. (b) Soul: You have a soul to soul connection, your spirit is connected, connecting to their story, having chemistry, feeling comfortable around the person, knowing that you can be with them and they may be who God made for you. (c) Intellectual. You feel like you and the person have a lot of things you can learn from each other such as information, ideas, experience, and knowledge. You are not bored speaking with the person.

(202) Every relationship is different and the secret to discovering what will make your relationship different is to learn how your partner to be is different. Stay away from comparing your relationship and partner with other people and forcing them to be who they are not.

(203) Communication is important. Women are typically communicative. Men are not. The times' men talk is

to woo a woman, need sex or food. Lack of communication causes you and your partner to drift apart from each other. There can never be too much communication. The more you do, the better your relationship gets. It is important to talk and share your thoughts. Invite your woman into your world, what you are thinking, and plans you have either finished or still in the making. Let her offer you advice, seek her opinion, and strategize together. Two heads are better than one. The advantage of regular communication with your partner is that it brings you closer spiritually, emotionally, and mentally. It makes your partner feel inclusive, helps you understand each other, strengthens your bond and chemistry, solidifies your friendship, and helps you finish each other's thought because you have spent so much time conversing, now you understand how he or she thinks and the kind of decisions they can make in a certain situation. Crawl out of your shell and have as much dialogue with your woman.

(204)   Single ladies be wise how you interpret a man's action. What turns a man's head does not always turn his heart and what gets his attention does not always earn his respect. Do not be a victim of lack of knowledge.

(205)   The modern-day approach to a successful marriage is the practice of relationship equity. To effectively execute it you must first understand the characteristics of

a 21st-century woman you are in a relationship with. Who is a 21st-century woman? She got it together, money alone cannot please her. You must satisfy her mind, soul, and body. She got high expectations, she is resourceful, her place is more than the bedroom and kitchen, and she loves and thinks differently from your mum. If you understood this as a man, your approach to your woman will be to strike equity balance so that you can maximize your family unit otherwise you will always be running into conflict and hence the divorce. What is relationship equity? Treating your partner, the way you would like to be treated; being fair to each other, and determining roles based on skill set, gifting, constraints, and not gender.

(206)   You are meant to cover each other as partners. There will be a trying time where money, education, wisdom, and knowledge that your partner possesses cannot solve the problem except prayers. There are issues you will run into in your life, marriage, family, ministry, career, business, health that the mundane things you have cannot solve except prayers. Get yourself a praying partner. Cultivate the habit to cover each other. A woman is made from a rib of her man. That rib covers the organs of the man. Likewise, the flesh of the man covers the rib (his wife). You are meant to cover each other as partners.

(207)   Singles come to me and want to know when a man or woman acts a certain way, what does it mean? what does it mean when he or she says a particular thing? There are many ways I can spin the answer and tell you the meaning of their actions. However, we need to first understand is the person the right person. Is he the person God made for you? Is she your rib? Is she your wife? Once the answer is yes, the rest is practical. Then we can start to work on the issues otherwise you will be working out issues with someone who is not the ideal mate for you.

(208)   Love is not at its best when all is good between you and the person you are dating. The true existence of love is demonstrated and revealed during adversity. You can only tell for sure if that person loves you when there is a challenge. For example: If you are sick, do they show kindness by volunteering to run to the store to get you medication, prepare food for you to eat, come to check up on you? If love is present, is that person you are dating willing to wait until you are ready for sex? If you love your partner, are you willing to demonstrate it by going through coaching/counseling or workshop to get help so that you can be a better man or woman for your partner? Love is seen and tested in adversity. God did not demonstrate his love by sending Jesus when things were initially good

in the garden. He did not send Jesus before the fall of men. He sent him when hell broke loose. When men's thoughts are full of evil. When men no longer respect the statutes of God. That is when He demonstrated his true love by sending his Son to reconcile us back to him, to set us back to the right path.

(209) If you and the person you are dating are constantly on a separate page, eventually it can lead to a break-up. The root cause of break-up is due to two different minds working on two different plans. They want different things and cannot come to a unified agreement. If you continue to operate like this with your partner and cannot decisively agree to be on one page, you will end up breaking up.

(210) What is affecting your communication is that you are not allowing each other to speak. Study shows women speak ~30,000 and men speak ~1/3 of that. If you keep interrupting your woman in the middle of her talk, eventually she will carry over the rest till the following day and that will be a Psunami conversation at that point. Men, please let your woman finish expressing herself. She is built to speak and express herself.

(211) Do you get upset with what your boyfriend or girlfriend says to you during an argument? This is a practical guide that can help you respond better: It is not

what Tyffany says to James that matters; It is what James says to James that can help create a better response. Whenever your partner says something disrespectful to you or gets you upset, have an internal dialogue within yourself that is positive to counteract what you are being told by your partner.

(212)   How can you choose your life partner? The way you can decipher your real partner from the one who is not is by having the spirit of discernment. If you do not have a spirit of discernment you will be led to choose your spouse by wrong motives, your wants instead of your needs. Spirit of discernment helps you to know what is in God's heart for you and not what is in your heart. It differentiates between what your flesh wants vs what the spirit of the Lord requires you to have to fulfill your assignment on earth. Work on having a spirit of discernment.

(213)   Are you having difficulty moving on from your past relationship? Are you still hurt by what the person did? Is your old relationship affecting the new one? Are you seeing patterns from your old relationship repeating in your new relationship? If yes, do you know why? Here is the reason: Though you left the relationship, however, all that relationship did not leave you especially if you were intimate and had a child together. It is like gluing two papers together. If you

tried to separate them, some parts of each paper will be on the other part. You cannot fully separate the two papers without leaving a mark. You can change jobs and not feel anything. You cannot change a serious relationship and not feel anything.

(214)   The best relationship you can have is first with God than with yourself. If those two are not strong, then the one with your partner will be weak.

(215)   Personality is as important as beauty. You cannot be happy having a beautiful woman with a nasty attitude. You will not want to go home to her. Likewise, you do not want to be attracted to a good-looking man with an abusive character. You will be living in fear for the rest of your life. Your aesthetic can attract them, but it is your character that will keep them.

(216)   Spending quality time is a sign that shows someone is in love with you. People spend time with what or whom they love. If the person you are seeing is always making excuses of not spending time with you, trust me you are not their priority and there is no love with who you are not prioritizing.

(217)   Your behavior and expectation of a new relationship are mostly hinged on the experience of your past relationship. To have a good relationship, you need to

evaluate and heal from your experience so that you do not treat your NEXT like your EX.

www.ingramcontent.com/pod-product-compliance
Lightning Source LLC
Chambersburg PA
CBHW050758240726

48654CB00008B/546